5/18

Earth Day

By EMMA CARLSON BERNE

Illustrations by MIKE BUNDAD

Music by ERIK KOSKINEN

CANTATA
LEARNING

WWW.CANTATALEARNING.COM

CANTATA LEARNING

Published by Cantata Learning
1710 Roe Crest Drive
North Mankato, MN 56003
www.cantatalearning.com

Library of Congress Cataloging-in-Publication Data
Names: Berne, Emma Carlson, author. | Bundad, Mike, illustrator. | Koskinen,
   Erik, composer.
Title: Earth day / by Emma Carlson Berne ; iIllustrated by Mike Bundad ;
   music by Erik Koskinen.
Description: North Mankato, MN : Cantata Learning, [2018] | Series: Holidays
   in rhythm and rhyme
Identifiers: LCCN 2017017512 (print) | LCCN 2017046232 (ebook) | ISBN
   9781684101542 (ebook) | ISBN 9781684102068 (hardcover : alk. paper) | ISBN
   9781684101917 (pbk. : alk. paper)
Subjects: LCSH: Earth Day--Juvenile literature. | Earth Day--Songs and music.
Classification: LCC GE195.5 (ebook) | LCC GE195.5 .B47 2018 (print) | DDC
   394.262--dc23
LC record available at https://lccn.loc.gov/2017017512

Book design and art direction, Tim Palin Creative
Editorial direction, Kellie M. Hultgren
Music direction, Elizabeth Draper
Music arranged and produced by Erik Koskinen

Printed in the United States of America in North Mankato, Minnesota.
122017   0378CGS18

TIPS TO SUPPORT LITERACY AT HOME

WHY READING AND SINGING WITH YOUR CHILD IS SO IMPORTANT

Daily reading with your child leads to increased academic achievement. Music and songs, specifically rhyming songs, are a fun and easy way to build early literacy and language development. Music skills correlate significantly with both phonological awareness and reading development. Singing helps build vocabulary and speech development. And reading and appreciating music together is a wonderful way to strengthen your relationship.

READ AND SING EVERY DAY!

TIPS FOR USING CANTATA LEARNING BOOKS AND SONGS DURING YOUR DAILY STORY TIME

1. As you sing and read, point out the different words on the page that rhyme. Suggest other words that rhyme.

2. Memorize simple rhymes such as Itsy Bitsy Spider and sing them together. This encourages comprehension skills and early literacy skills.

3. Use the questions in the back of each book to guide your singing and storytelling.

4. Read the included sheet music with your child while you listen to the song. How do the music notes correlate to the words of the song?

5. Sing along on the go and at home. Access music by scanning the QR code on each Cantata book, or by using the included CD. You can also stream or download the music for free to your computer, smartphone, or mobile device.

Devoting time to daily reading shows that you are available for your child. Together, you are building language, literacy, and listening skills.

Have fun reading and singing!

Earth Day is in the spring. In the 1970s, people found out that Earth was getting too dirty. They made a holiday to remind others to keep Earth clean.

On April 22, people do things to help Earth. Some people plant trees. Others pick up **litter**. On Earth Day, people make promises. They promise to **recycle** their trash. They ask factories to promise not to **pollute** the air and water.

To learn more about Earth Day, turn the page and sing along!

paper

5

Grab a shovel, find a rake,
get all the trash cans you can take.

Let's go outside,
   let's plant a tree.
Come on, it's Earth Day,
   can't you see?

7

This is our Earth! We breathe this air.
We live on this soil. That's why we care!

9

Nuts for squirrels
and twigs for nests,
trees give the things
animals love best.

Get a new **sapling**, plant it in dirt,
give it some water, and let the sun work.

This is our Earth!
We breathe this air.
We live on this soil.
That's why we care!

Look, there's litter all over the place:
plastic bags, pop cans, and ugly waste.

Pick up trash and plant something new.
Today we are Earth's cleanup crew!

This is our Earth! We breathe this air.
We live on this soil. That's why we care!

Each year we **celebrate** special times,
like Halloween and the Fourth of July.

April twenty-second is Earth's holiday.
Our planet's beautiful—let's keep it that way!

This is our Earth! We breathe this air.
We live on this soil. That's why we care!

SONG LYRICS
Earth Day

Grab a shovel, find a rake,
get all the trash cans you can take.

Let's go outside, let's plant a tree.
Come on, it's Earth Day, can't you see?

This is our Earth! We breathe this air.
We live on this soil. That's why we care!

Nuts for squirrels and twigs for nests,
trees give the things animals love best.

Get a new sapling, plant it in dirt,
give it some water, and let the sun work.

This is our Earth! We breathe this air.
We live on this soil. That's why we care!

Look, there's litter all over the place:
plastic bags, pop cans, and ugly waste.

Pick up trash and plant something new.
Today we are Earth's cleanup crew!

This is our Earth! We breathe this air.
We live on this soil. That's why we care!

Each year we celebrate special times,
like Halloween and the Fourth of July.

April twenty-second is Earth's holiday.
Our planet's beautiful—let's keep it
 that way!

This is our Earth! We breathe this air.
We live on this soil. That's why we care!

Earth Day

Americana
Erik Koskinen

Verse 2
Nuts for squirrels and twigs for nests,
trees give the things animals love best.
Get a new sapling, plant it in dirt,
give it some water, and let the sun work.

Chorus

Verse 3
Look, there's litter all over the place:
plastic bags, pop cans, and ugly waste.
Pick up trash and plant something new.
Today we are Earth's cleanup crew!

Chorus

Verse 4
Each year we celebrate special times,
like Halloween and the Fourth of July.
April twenty-second is Earth's holiday.
Our planet's beautiful—let's keep it that way!

Chorus

GLOSSARY

celebrate–to do something special to mark an important day

litter–trash that is on the ground outside

pollute–to make air, water, or soil dirty

sapling–a baby tree

recycle–to use metal, plastic, glass, or paper over again, instead of throwing it away

GUIDED READING ACTIVITIES

1. Why are Earth Day celebrations important? What do these celebrations remind us to think about?

2. Planting trees and picking up litter are two ways this book suggests to celebrate Earth Day. What are two more things you can do to help keep our Earth clean?

3. On Earth Day we think of our oceans, our mountains, plants, and animals. What is your favorite outdoor place or animal? Why do you like this place or this animal?

TO LEARN MORE

Jiménez, Vita. *Make Every Day Earth Day!* North Mankato, MN: Cantata Learning, 2017.

Lennon, Julian, and Bart Davis. *Touch the Earth*. New York: Sky Pony Press, 2017.

Parr, Todd. *The Earth Book*. New York: Little, Brown, 2010.